Politics 101

What your elected officials don't want you to know

Stephen B. Fraser

Preface

The other day I was sitting in my local coffee shop reading a book and enjoying my coffee when the two people at the next table started talking rather loudly about politics. While I sat there trying to not listen to their conversation I quickly found myself enthralled but what they were saying.

One talked about how the economy is never going to get back on track because of the Republicans. The other talked about how the Democrats just want to spend more money and run us further into debt. This conversation continued on for several minutes till finally both men finished their coffees and left. While I sat there eavesdropping on their conversation. I noticed several people in the coffee shop listening and nodding when they agreed with a comment or shake their head if they disagreed. Throughout the rest of that day I pondered on the misconceptions that both men had. As well as how politics is the one thing very few people know a lot about.

The following day I sat down and started writing this book. I figured it would be about 20 or 30 pages long and relatively a quick read. But the more I researched the more I had to put into this book. The result is what you see sitting in front of you know. While I don't expect everyone that reads this to see things as I do. I hope to make you see how things are done and hope to clear up and misconceptions you might have about the government as well.

I hope to shed some light on politics in general. First of all I am not a Political Science Major, but I have taken basic government classes in college so I feel that I can be objective. Second while I do affiliate myself with a particular political party it is my attempt not to let that sway this book to one side or the other. Third this is really designed as an overview of the political system not a complete and concise collection of politics as a whole. I hope you enjoy this as much as I have enjoyed writing it.

Note - all items in this book remain the sole intellectual property of their respectful owners. When it was possible sources were provided.

Chapter 1

A Little Bit of Background

The United States is the world's oldest surviving federation. It is a constitutional republic and representative democracy. The government is regulated by a system of checks and balances defined by the U.S. Constitution. In the American system, citizens are subject to three levels of government. These are federal, state, and local. At the local government level duties are commonly split between county and municipal governments.

The federal government is composed of three branches:

Legislative: The bicameral Congress, made up of the Senate and the House of Representatives. They are responsible for making federal law, declaring war, approving treaties, controls the power of the purse, and has the power of impeachment.

Executive: The President is the commander-in-chief of the military, can veto legislative bills before they become law, and appoints the members of the Cabinet, and other officers.

Judicial: The Supreme Court, whose judges are appointed by the President with Senate approval. They are responsible for interpreting laws and overturning those they find unconstitutional.

The House of Representatives has 435 voting members, each representing a congressional district for a two-year term. House seats are apportioned among the states by population every tenth year. As of the 2000 census, seven states have the minimum of one representative, while California, the most populous state, has fifty-three. The Senate has 100 members with each state having two senators, elected at-large to six-year terms; one third of Senate seats are up for election every other year.

The President serves a four-year term and may be elected to the office for no more than two terms. The president is not elected by direct vote, but by an Electoral College system in which the determining votes are apportioned to the states and the District of Columbia.

The Supreme Court, is led by the Chief Justice of the United States, has nine members, who serve for life. All laws and governmental procedures are subject to judicial review and any law ruled in violation of the Constitution is voided.

The state governments are structured in a similar fashion. The Governor (chief executive) of each state is directly elected. Some state judges and cabinet officers are appointed by the Governor of the respective state, while others are elected by popular vote. Each State may have its own State Constitution and Laws separate from Federal Laws.

The original text of the Constitution establishes the structure and responsibilities of the federal government and its relationship with the individual states. Amendments to the Constitution require the approval of three-fourths of the states. The Constitution has been amended twenty-seven times; the first ten amendments, which make up the Bill of Rights, and the Fourteenth Amendment form the central basis of Americans' individual rights.

This you probably already know. However that was just the beginning. That was the way our government was set up and since we have done nothing but try to tweak it to make it better, or in some cases worse. Let's take one simple thing like the dollar bill. The value of a 1775 Dollar compared to today would be $30. Originally Members of Congress were paid Six Dollars ($6) a day while in session equivalent to about One Hundred and Forty Dollars ($140) today. So a in a year a congressman in 1780 would make $2190.00. Equivalent today that would be approximately $48,890.00. **George Washington** was paid a salary of $25,000 a year from 1789 to 1797 as the first president of the United States. The current salary of the president has recently been doubled to $400,000, to go with a $50,000 expense account, a generous pension and several other benefits.

We don't want to get ahead of ourselves. Congress is a group of elected officials whom we the people have elected to act on our behalf. I believe that when our nation was forming that was happening. However I think we have gone astray somewhere down the line.

Just about nightly when you watch the news there is something on about the government or the president and what they are doing or not doing. Then if its and election year we get bombarded with ads about this candidate and that candidate and how they are the best thing for us and why we should vote for them. If it is a presidential election year well it's even worse. Usually they start campaigning a year before the election. For example we are going to be electing a new President or re-electing the current President on November 6, 2012. However the candidates started campaigning back about January 15, 2011. So by the time we get to November we are all so sick and tired of the mudslinging that we just want it all over with.

Chapter 2

Congress

I use to think it would be great to be a U.S. Congressman, you get to work in Washington D.C., and you get a great office, Interns that do anything you say, and a good salary to boot. Currently there are 435 members in the House of Representatives, each representing a congressional district. Each one is up for election or re-election every two years. There are 100 members of the Senate. That is 2 Senators for each State. Senators are elected to 6 year terms. Neither the House nor Senate has term limits like the Presidency does. There for you can have Senators and Representatives that can serve till death and some have.

	Senator	Dates of Service	Length of service
1	Robert C. Byrd (D-WV)	1/3/59 to 5/28/10	51 years, 5 months, 26 days
2	Daniel K. Inouye (D-HI)	1/3/63 to present	48 years, 4 months
3	Strom Thurmond (R-SC)	12/24/54 to 1/3/03	47 years, 5 months, 8 days
4	Edward M. Kennedy (D-MA)	11/7/62 to 8/25/09	46 years, 9 months, 19 days
5	Carl T. Hayden (D-AZ)	3/4/27 to 1/3/69	41 years, 9 months, 30 days
6	John Stennis (D-MS)	11/5/47 to 1/3/89	41 years, 1 month, 29 days
7	Ted Stevens (R-AK)	12/24/68 to 1/3/09	40 years, 10 days
8	Ernest F. Hollings (D-SC)	11/9/66 to 1/3/05	38 years, 1 month 25 days
9	Richard B. Russell (D-GA)	1/3/33 to 1/21/71	38 years, 19 days
10	Russell Long (D-LA)	12/31/48 to 1/3/87	38 years, 3 days

Source: htttp://www.senate.gov

The list above is just Senators however currently in the House of Representatives there is this list.

	Representative	Consecutive Terms	Length of service
1	John Dingell (D-MI)	29 Terms	59 years
2	John Conyers, Jr. (D-MI)	24 Terms	47 years
3	David Obey (D-WI)	21 Terms	42 years
4	Charles Rangel (D-NY)	21 Terms	41 years
5	C.W. (Bill) Young (R-FL)	21 Terms	41 years
6	Fortney Stark (D-CA)	20 Terms	39 years
7	George Miller (D-CA)	19 Terms	39 years
8	Henry Waxman (D-CA)	19 Terms	37 years
9	John Murtha (D-PA)	18 Terms	37 years
10	James L. Oberstar (D-MN)	18 Terms	36 years

Source:

http://en.wikipedia.org/wiki/List_of_members_of_the_United_States_Congress_by_longevity_of_service

I guess it pays to be a democrat in the House of Representatives when it comes to re-election time. It also bears to mention that on both lists the names highlighted in yellow are currently sitting Senators and Representatives.

So what exactly do these Senators and Representatives do for us? The legislative branch is the one charged with creating the laws that hold our society together. The Constitution established congress in Article I. Congress is the collective legislative body made up of the Senate and the House. While the primary function of these two bodies is to write, debate and pass bills and to send them on to the president for his approval or veto. If the president gives his approval to a bill, it immediately becomes law. However, if the president vetoes the bill, Congress may override the presidential veto with a two-thirds majority in both houses. Congress may also rewrite a bill in hopes to get the President's approval. When legislation is vetoed it is sent back to the house or senate chamber where it originated from for reworking. However, if the President receives a bill and does nothing within 10 days while Congress is in session, the bill automatically becomes law.

Congress can also investigate pressing national issues, it is charged with supervising and providing a balance for the executive and judicial branches as well. It has the authority to declare war. It has the power to coin money. They also regulate interstate and foreign commerce and trade. Congress also is responsible for maintaining the military. However the President serves as its commander in chief.

In order to balance the concerns of smaller but more populated states against those of larger but more sparsely populated ones. The framers of the Constitution formed two separate chambers. The Senate has 100 members, with each state allowed two representatives, regardless of size or population. The House of Representatives currently has 435 members, with each state's representation dependent upon its population. Each member of the House represents a specific geographic district within the state, while senators represent their whole state.

While each house has some specific duties they are also different as well. The House can initiate laws that require people to pay taxes and can decide whether public officials should be tried if accused of a crime. Representatives are elected to two-year terms. House leadership rests with the speaker of the house. This is usually a senior member of the majority party. The speaker applies House rules and refers bills to specific House committees for review. The speaker is also third in line to the presidency, after the vice president. There are additional leadership positions, the majority and minority leaders that monitor legislative activity on the floor, and the majority and minority whips that ensure that House members vote according to their respective parties' positions.

The Senate can confirm or reject any treaties the president establishes with other nations and is also responsible for confirming presidential appointments of Cabinet members, federal judges and foreign ambassadors. The Senate also tries any federal official accused of a crime after the House votes to impeach that official. Senators are elected to six-year terms. The vice president presides over the Senate and has the right to cast his vote in the event of a tie.

During the Constitutional Convention, Benjamin Franklin considered proposing that elected government officials not be paid for their service. Other Founding Fathers, however, decided otherwise. From 1789 to 1855, members of Congress received only a daily payment of $6.00 while in session, except for a period from December 1815 to March 1817, when they received $1,500 a year. Members began receiving an annual salary in 1855, when they were paid $3,000 per year.

So how much do your congressmen and women make for serving their respective voters?

The current salary (2011) for rank-and-file members of the House and Senate is $174,000 per year. While members are free to turn down pay increases this rarely happens. However, recently some members have chosen to do so. Leaders of the House and Senate are paid a higher salary than rank-and-file members.

House Leadership

Speaker of the House - $223,500

Majority Leader - $193,400

Minority Leader - $193,400

Senate Leadership

Majority Party Leader - $193,400

Minority Party Leader - $193,400

A cost-of-living-adjustment (COLA) increase takes effect annually unless Congress votes to not accept it. As to date this has never happened.

Many people believe that Members of Congress do not pay into Social Security. This is however not the case. Prior to 1984, neither Members of Congress nor any other federal civil service employee paid Social Security taxes. Of course, they were also not eligible to receive Social Security benefits. Members of Congress and other federal employees were instead covered by a separate pension plan called the Civil Service Retirement System. The 1983 amendments to the Social Security Act required federal employees first hired after 1983 to participate in Social Security. These amendments also required all Members of Congress to participate in Social

Security as of January 1, 1984, regardless of when they first entered Congress. The result was the Federal Employees' Retirement System Act of 1986.

Members of Congress receive retirement and health benefits under the same plans available to other federal employees. They become vested after five years of full participation. Members elected since 1984 are covered by the Federal Employees' Retirement System (FERS). Those elected prior to 1984 were covered by the Civil Service Retirement System (CSRS). In 1984 all members were given the option of remaining with CSRS or switching to FERS.

As it is for all other federal employees, congressional retirement is funded through taxes and the participants' contributions. Members of Congress under FERS contribute 1.3 percent of their salary into the FERS retirement plan and pay 6.2 percent of their salary in Social Security taxes.

Members of Congress are not eligible for a pension until they reach the age of 50, but only if they've completed 20 years of service. Members are eligible at any age after completing 25 years of service or after they reach the age of 62. Please also note that Members of Congress have to serve at least 5 years to even receive a pension.

The amount of a congressperson's pension depends on the years of service and the average of the highest 3 years of his or her salary. By law, the starting amount of a Member's retirement annuity may not exceed 80% of his or her final salary.

According to the Congressional Research Service, 413 retired Members of Congress were receiving federal pensions based fully or in part on their congressional service as of Oct. 1, 2006. Of this number, 290 had retired under CSRS and were receiving an average annual pension of $60,972. A total of 123 Members had retired with service under both CSRS and FERS or with service under FERS only. Their average annual pension was $35,952 in 2006.

But what about these wonderful benefits that includes...

Free parking: Not only do members of Congress receive parking on Capitol Hill, but they also receive free private parking spots at the two nearby airport, Reagan National and Dulles airport.

Office Space: Members of congress receive a generous sized office on Capitol Hill. Free of charge, the tax payers pay for everything, heat, air conditioning, security, janitorial, phone system, secretarial, and even the congressman's staff.

Perks from Lobbyists: Despite a slew of ethics regulations regarding gifts from lobbyists, Members of Congress are still able to use their lobbyist ties to get into events that regular people simply do not have access to. For example, if a Member of Congress wanted a prime ticket to a sold-out event, he could still get that ticket from lobbyists he's close with, as long as the face value of the ticket is reimbursed by the Member. However, this money doesn't have to come from the Member's pocket, but instead can come from the usually deep campaign account, which usually contains money from lobbyists and their associated PACs.

Free Travel and Trips: Want to take a "fact finding" trip to France? Not a problem if you are a member of Congress, so long as it's "business" related. Just join a committee and chances are you will need to carry out one of these STRICTLY-BUSINESS-TRIPS overseas at least once.

Last year, the Congressional Research Council found that it is nearly impossible for the public to find out which Congressional members make trips and where they go. What's more, current laws don't impose any spending limits on these government trips. The U.S. Treasury simply refills the travel funds on an "as-needed" basis.

Additionally, Congress members get to travel between D.C. and their home district for free as often as they like.

Days Off: While most Americans get one day off for Memorial Day and sometimes Presidents Day, members of Congress get the entire week off. However, Congress doesn't like to call these vacation days, but instead call them "District Work Periods," even though there is nothing requiring them to be in their district during those times. Congress also gets a number of additional recesses, some lasting as long as a month. When all that trip-taking wears them down, members of Congress can always fall back on their vacation time. Out of 260 working days in a year, Congress only works 137 of them.

In the first 42 weeks of 2011, Congress members worked an average of 2.67 days per week. Amazingly, that's actually a better attendance rate than usual -- the last two years, our legislative branch only worked 111 days.

Free Postage: Members of Congress can send Newsletters, official correspondence and letters to anyone even overseas for free. When you get that wonder full mail box full of "What I'm doing for you in Washington" Newsletter and letters from your congressman you are throwing your money away. The Tax payers bought all of that from the printing straight down to the mailing.

So let's see your Congressman makes $174,000 per year, and the average American's annual income is $49,900. That's three times what the average American worker makes! Maybe Congress should be paid minimum wage and give back some of their benefits. Maybe then we wouldn't have such a huge debt problem.

So how do we get laws?

Anybody who grew up in the late 70's and 80's and watched cartoons on Saturday morning, will probably remember the "School House Rock" skit about this. As a matter of fact it is running through my head right now as I write this.

Well it all starts with a bill…

Introduction of Bills.　Bills can begin in either the House or the Senate. Different versions of a bill can begin in both chambers concurrently.

- Bills can only be introduced by members of Congress.
- Many bills originate in the executive branch and are introduced by a congressional sponsor.
- New bills are numbered and sent to the appropriate committee.

Committee Action.　The bill comes under its most intense scrutiny while in committee, and many bills die in committee.

- The bill is considered either by the full committee or a subcommittee.
- After hearings and study to "mark up" the bill, the full committee votes on a recommendation to the House or Senate.
- The committee may order a "clean bill," with a new number, to be introduced.

Floor Action.　Next, the bill appears before the entire House or Senate. The two chambers have different procedures for floor debate.

House:

- The House Rules Committee regulates debate for each bill, issuing the "rule" for the bill.
- Members can speak on a bill for a set period of time, as specified in the "rule."
- To speed debate on some bills, the House meets as the Committee of the Whole, which has different rules for floor debate. The Committee of the Whole can amend a bill, but cannot pass it.

Senate:

- Senate debate is unlimited. Senators may speak at any length on any topic.
- Any senator can stop debate with a "filibuster."
- Debate can be closed by unanimous consent, or by invoking "cloture," which requires a three-fifths majority (at least 60 votes) of the entire Senate.

Second Chamber. Once one chamber has voted to pass a bill, the other chamber may:

- Pass it with the language intact.
- Refer it to a committee for scrutiny or alteration.
- Reject the entire bill, informing the other chamber of its actions, or

- Ignore the bill, while continuing to work on its own version of the legislation.

Conference. When the two chambers pass differing versions of legislation, the bill goes to conference - the "third chamber" of Congress.

- Conferees for the House and Senate committees that worked on the bill meet together to work out a compromise.
- Conferees are not allowed to write new legislation; they must work within the boundaries of the differences in the House and Senate bills.
- When the conferees have reached agreement, they submit a report of their recommendations to each chamber for approval.

The President. The Speaker of the House and the President of the Senate both sign the approved bill and send it to the president, who then has four options.

- If the president signs and dates the bill, it becomes law.
- If Congress is in session, and the president does not sign the bill within 10 days, the bill becomes law without his signature.

- The president may "veto" the entire bill. The bill goes back to Congress for a second vote, in which it must get a two-thirds majority of votes in each chamber in order to become law.
- If Congress adjourns within 10 days of giving the bill to the president, and he does not sign it, the bill dies. This is called a "pocket veto."

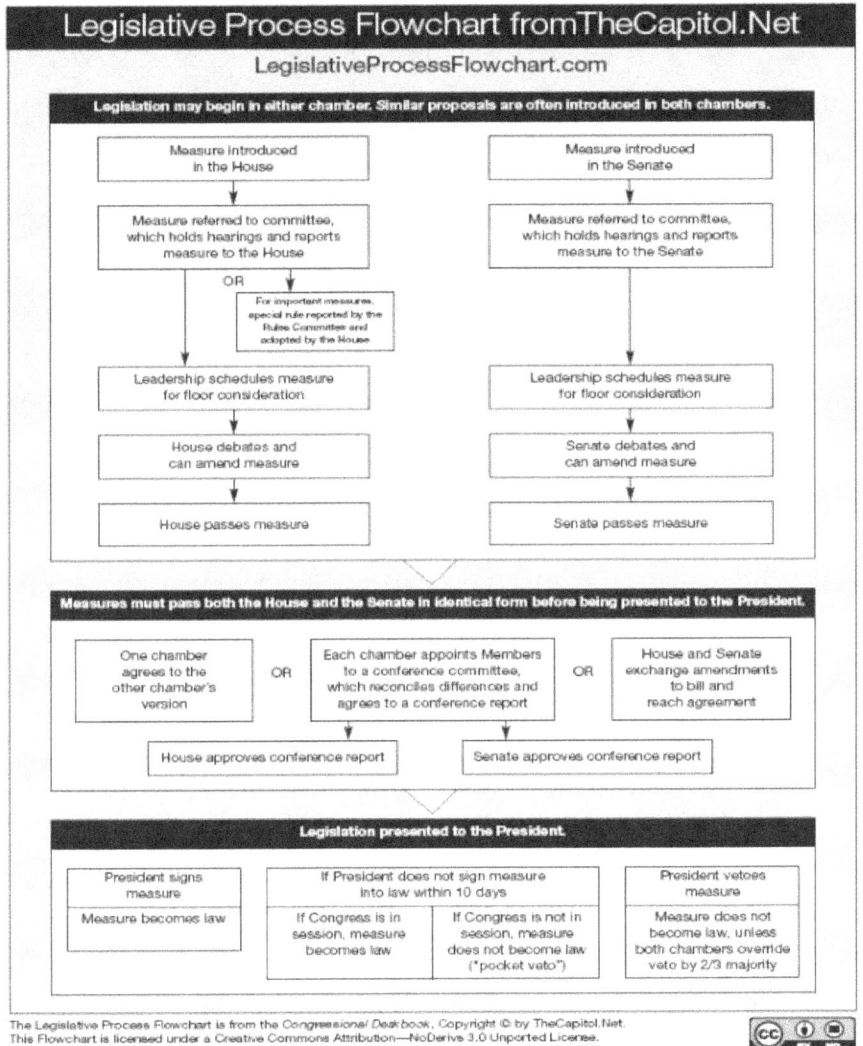

Legislative Process Flowchart fromTheCapitol.Net

LegislativeProcessFlowchart.com

Legislation may begin in either chamber. Similar proposals are often introduced in both chambers.

Measure introduced in the House	Measure introduced in the Senate

Measure referred to committee, which holds hearings and reports measure to the House

OR

For important measures, special rule reported by the Rules Committee and adopted by the House

Measure referred to committee, which holds hearings and reports measure to the Senate

Leadership schedules measure for floor consideration

Leadership schedules measure for floor consideration

House debates and can amend measure

Senate debates and can amend measure

House passes measure

Senate passes measure

Measures must pass both the House and the Senate in identical form before being presented to the President.

One chamber agrees to the other chamber's version

OR

Each chamber appoints Members to a conference committee, which reconciles differences and agrees to a conference report

OR

House and Senate exchange amendments to bill and reach agreement

House approves conference report

Senate approves conference report

Legislation presented to the President.

President signs measure

Measure becomes law

If President does not sign measure into law within 10 days

If Congress is in session, measure becomes law

If Congress is not in session, measure does not become law ("pocket veto")

President vetoes measure

Measure does not become law, unless both chambers override veto by 2/3 majority

The Legislative Process Flowchart is from the Congressional Deskbook, Copyright © by TheCapitol.Net. This Flowchart is licensed under a Creative Commons Attribution-NoDerivs 3.0 Unported License. Permissions beyond the scope of this license may be available: www.thecapitol.net, 202-678-1600.

So let's say we want a law that makes driving while talking on the cell phone without a hands free device illegal. So our Congressman proposes a bill that says "It shall be illegal to operate a motor vehicle while talking on a cellular phone." The proposed Bill goes into committee. In committee it gets debated and changed buy other congressmen who may or may not have been influenced by lobbyists, or constituents. And then comes out of committee representing something like…"It shall be illegal to operate a motor vehicle while talking or texting on a cellular phone between the hours of 7:00 AM and 7:00 PM." The House debates the bill on the house floor, this can generate even more modifying of the bill, or even result in other things getting added to the bill. The Bill passes the House vote and heads to the Senate. The Senate debates the bill and can even make changes to the bill as well. However, if this happens then when the bill passes the Senate vote it would have to go back to the House to be voted on again.

Finally after all of this the bill goes to the President to be signed. The President has two choices he can read and accept the Bill and sign it into Law, or he can Veto the Bill. Now we can all assume that the President reads every word of every page of every bill that crosses his desk. I personally don't think so. I believe that the President has other people that read the bills and give him the highlights. This is why in the past we as the Tax payers have paid $500 for Hammers for military construction workers, and $1000 for portable toilets for military airplanes.

However let's say the President does read the whole bill word for word and he likes everything but one line that says "Upon passage of the bill California will be given an additional $450,000 to pay for added police to cite drivers using cellular phones after the law goes into effect." Now the rest of the Bill could be great and the public is asking for this kind of law. But the President thinks that this part is wrong and shouldn't be in the Bill. His only choice is to veto the whole bill, or sign it into Law and give California the money. This is why the President needs a **Line Item Veto** Power.

Almost every State Governor in the United States has the power to **Line Item Veto** parts of a bill. But yet we don't give the President the power to do this. So maybe we should ask ourselves, **who really runs the country?**

In summary Congress is responsible for making the laws, such as Bank robbery is Illegal. Controlling the purse, because the government can't spend money if congress doesn't say it can. Investigate pressing national issues, such as did Bill Clinton get a blowjob in the oval office from Monica Lewinski. It has the authority to declare war, Such as Afghanistan and Iraq. It is responsible for maintaining the military, deciding how big our military needs to be.

All of this and you get a great paycheck and maybe some of the best benefits of anyone in the United States. Maybe I will reconsider running for congress myself...

Chapter 3

The Presidency

The Presidency of the United States has got to be the hardest job in the world. First of all I will say it's the one job I will never want. First of all you get very little respect cause no matter what you do someone isn't going to be happy with it. Second there is always some crisis somewhere that requires your attention. Third despite what people may think you have very little power at all. So what does the President really do?

The Constitution assigns the president two roles: Commander in Chief of the armed forces and chief executive of the federal government. As Commander in Chief, the president has the authority to send troops into combat, and is the only one who can decide whether to use nuclear weapons. However Congress is the only one that can declare war.

As chief executive, he enforces laws, treaties, and court rulings. He develops federal policies and prepares the national budget. He can appoint federal officials (providing Congress confirms it). He also approves or vetoes acts of Congress and grants pardons.

So what does it take to become President? First, you need to be a native-born U.S. citizen (or those born abroad, but only to parents who were both citizens of the U.S.) Second, you must also be at least 35 years of age to be president. John F. Kennedy was the youngest person to be elected president at the age of 43 when he was inaugurated in 1961. Ronald Reagan was the oldest president at the age of 77 when he left office. Third, you must live in the United States for at least 14 years to be president. These are the only explicit criteria in the Constitution. It's easier to be a congressman and you don't have term limits!

The annual salary of the president of the United States is $400,000 per year, including a $50,000 expense allowance. Under the Former Presidents Act, each former president is paid a lifetime, taxable pension that is equal to the annual rate of basic pay for the head of an executive federal department $199,700.

Former Presidents and their spouses, widows, and minor children are entitled to treatment in military hospitals. Former presidents and their dependents also have the option of enrolling in private health insurance plans at their own expense. Former presidents are traditionally granted state funerals with military honors. Details of the funeral are based on the wishes of the former president's family.

Former presidents who entered office before January 1, 1997 and their spouses get Secret Service protection for life, unless they choose to decline it. Surviving spouses of former presidents get secret service protection until they remarry. Former presidents who entered office after January 1, 1997 and their spouses get Secret Service protection for a maximum of 10 years. A spouse's 10-year protection ends upon divorce, remarriage, or the death of the former president. In the event of the death of a serving president, the spouse gets Secret Service protection for one year. In addition, the Secretary of Homeland Security can authorize temporary protection at any time. Former President George W. Bush is the first President to have his protection limited to 10 years after leaving office.

Protection for a former president's children is available to them until the age of 16 or for a period not to exceed 10 years, whichever occurs first. In addition, the Presidential Threat Protection Act of 2000 granted the Secret Service additional authority to investigate threats against former presidents and their families.

The Secret Service also provides protective services to the vice president, (or other individuals next in order of succession to the Office of the President), the president-elect and vice president-elect, and the immediate families of those individuals. In regard to presidential campaign, the Secret Service is authorized by law to protect:

Major presidential and vice presidential candidates and their spouses within 120 days of a general presidential election. As defined in statute, the term "major presidential and vice presidential candidates" means those individuals identified as such by the Secretary of Homeland Security after consultation with an advisory committee.

The Secret Service provides protection for major candidates, unless declined. The Secret Service has no role in determining who is to be considered a major candidate. The Secretary of the Homeland Security determines who qualifies as a major candidate and when such protection should commence. This determination is made in consultation with an advisory committee comprised of the following individuals:

- Speaker of the House
- House Minority Whip
- Senate Majority Leader
- Senate Minority Leader
- One additional member chosen by the committee

While the President may be the top official in the government he has very little power compared to the rest of the government. For instance the President cannot one day wake up and say ok everybody in America gets healthcare. He has to make his pitch to the Congress, which is usually done in the form of a speech to the American people. Then wait for congress to hammer out a bill that makes it happen. Usually the result is a lot different than what the President proposes. Which we saw evidence of in the President Obama healthcare reform battle in 2009.

Being the President is not really an easy job either like I said in the beginning of the chapter. I am sure that the President has a lot of sleepless nights and concerns. Trying to be the leader of this great nation in its self has to be taxing. It is no wonder that when you look at pictures of Presidents when they enter office, and then compare them to ones when they leave office you can see just how much they have aged.

Also it is interesting to see that the President is always the one who gets blamed for everything that goes wrong with the country. If the President has a lack luster first term he is almost reassured that he won't be re-elected. Sometimes how things are handled can cause a President a re-election bid. Former President Jimmy Carter often said that one of the reasons he lost a second term was because of the handling of the Iran Hostage Crisis. However some issues can also help a President to win re-election. The best example was 9-11 and how former President George W. Bush handled it that helped him win re-election despite it having happened three years prior to the re-election.

So why is it we blame the President for everything when the people we should be getting rid of are the Congressmen? The answer is simply that the President is the most visible person we see. I can count on one hand how many times I have seen my Congressman. Of that half were during his re-election bid. I don't get those what I'm doing for you newsletters till he wants me to re-elect him.

Chapter 4

What is really going on?

So let's look at the parts as they relate to us as a people. We elect congressmen to protect our rights in Government and to look out for our best interests. The problem is that my best interest and your best interest could be totally different. We could see eye to eye on one issue, but have totally different views on a separate issue. So how is our congressmen supposed to know what to do? That is where the problem is. If we don't talk to our congressmen they can't effectively work for us. So at this point now you're sitting there thinking why are they going to listen to me. The answer is because they want to be re-elected. More importantly they like getting paid.

In Washington, DC there are several ways to get paid. Lobbyists use funds to influence Congressmen to back certain bills. Companies use congressional contacts to bend congressmen to support a bill or to add or remove a part of a bill they don't like. But you are saying to yourself but they have to disclose those "Donations" right? Well yes in theory they do. But if say Blue Cross/Blue Shield Insurance Company wants a few Senators to vote against a piece of legislation that they don't like they just write a bunch of "campaign contribution" checks to these same Senators. Then suggest that they just vote against this bill. Inevitably somebody always thinks this is ok, no matter how you look at it I think it is corruption.

So how did your congressman get to Washington to begin with? More than likely he spent more money than his opponent. Also because his name was out there more, and likely it was more positive than negative. A majority of people voted for him. Then the very first priority on his list when he got to office was to make sure he gets re-elected. But if you ask people why they voted for someone over someone else you will get a myriad of answers. Below are some of my favorites.

- He is a rancher and he will work to protect the American farmer.
- He is cute and has trusting eyes.

- He's a true family man.
- He is a Mormon. (Heard that in Idaho and Utah)
- He is a Democrat (or Republican).
- My all-time personal favorite…
- She looks cute and you know somewhere there are nude pictures of her that will come out if she gets elected. (Incidentally this was said about Sarah Palin when she was running as McCain's VP)

The last one kills me because I think about how many men voted for McCain just for that reason. Sadly though we may never know if that is true or not.

Now let's talk about political parties. Typically we have two parties in the United States Democrat or Republican. However in the last few years a couple more have started to gain more support.

The Democratic Party-

The Democratic Party evolved from Anti-Federalist factions that opposed the fiscal policies of Alexander Hamilton in the early 1790s. Thomas Jefferson and James Madison organized these factions into the Democratic-Republican Party. The party favored states' rights and strict adherence to the Constitution; it opposed a national bank and wealthy, moneyed interests. The Democratic-Republican Party ascended to power in the election of 1800.

After the War of 1812, the party's chief rival, the Federalist Party disbanded. Democratic-Republicans split over the choice of a successor to President James Monroe, and the party faction that supported many of the old Jeffersonian principles, led by Andrew Jackson and Martin Van Buren, became the Democratic Party.[1]

The Republican Party-

---

[1] Source: http://en.wikipedia.org/wiki/Democratic_Party_(United_States)

Founded in Northern States in 1854 by anti-slavery activists, modernizers, ex-Whigs and ex-Free Soilers, the Republican Party quickly became the principal opposition to the dominant Democratic Party and the briefly popular Know Nothing Party. The main cause was opposition to the Kansas–Nebraska Act, which repealed the Missouri Compromise by which slavery was kept out of Kansas. The Republicans saw the expansion of slavery as a great evil. The first public meeting where the name "Republican" was suggested for a new anti-slavery party was held on March 20, 1854 in a schoolhouse in Ripon, Wisconsin.

The first official party convention was held on July 6, 1854 in Jackson, Michigan. By 1858, the Republicans dominated nearly all Northern states. The Republican Party first came to power in 1860 with the election of Lincoln to the Presidency and Republicans in control of Congress and the northern states. It oversaw the saving of the union, the destruction of slavery, and the provision of equal rights to all men in the American Civil War and Reconstruction, 1861-1877[2]

The Independent Party-

---

[2] Source: http://en.wikipedia.org/wiki/Republican_Party_(United_States)

It is hard to find any actual history on how the Independent part got founded. Even harder is to find how they are structured belief wise. But it is safe to assume that as we progress that they will become a bigger part of our governmental party structure.

So we have heard about Right and Left wing right? So what does that mean? Basically the Right Wing is considered to be Conservative. And the Left wing is considered to be Liberal. (The Independents tend to believe they are in the middle.)

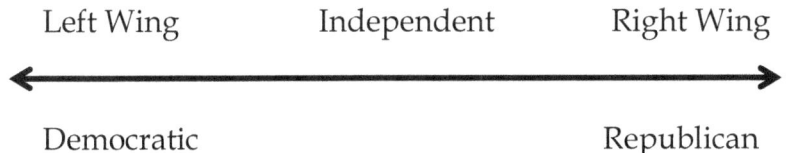

Left Wing   Independent   Right Wing

Democratic   Republican

Where you are on the line depends on your political views and what you believe in as being right and wrong. For instance let's look at abortion. If you are of the mindset that is a woman's choice (not typically a religious view) you would be considered Pro-Choice which would put you more on the Right Wing side. Now if you are of the mindset that life begins at conception and abortion is murder (typically the religious view) then you are Pro-Life and would be considered Left Wing. I personally don't believe in trying to divide a person's views into one of two groups. Mostly because I believe in some issues where I am Right Wing or I might fall into the Left Wing. Some things I am liberal about while others I am more conservative. Finally I might be Republican thinking about some issues or I might be more Democratic thinking in other issues. So if the question is are you a Democrat or a Republican the answer is yes I am.

The other problem with parties is what I have heard referred to as the "Dyed in the wool Syndrome." This is typically more seen in older voters. This is where someone is of the thinking "The Democrats are for the Working people. I am a Democrat and I'm a working person so I should vote for a Democrat." First of all if all, if all Democrats are working people I am grossly underpaid. (See Chapter 2) Because, eight of the longest serving Senate members and nine of the longest serving House Members are Democrats. Let us take Representative John Dingell who has been in the House 59 years, and he makes roughly $174,000 per year. In 59 years he has made a total of **$10,266,000**. Yes that's right that is **Ten Million Two Hundred Sixty Six Thousand Dollars**. Now compare that to the average American worker who only makes $49,900 annually. In the same 59 year period they only make **$2,944,100.** That seems to be a huge divide between the two.

Another problem with the "Dyed in the wool syndrome" voters is that they refuse to see the other side of an issue. I am sure everyone knows someone who voted what is called party line. That is where you look at the ballot and say ok I'm a Republican (or Democrat) and vote only for the Republican candidates straight down the form. That is not voting that isn't even voting on issue. That is simply put blind leading the blind. "Dyed in the wool syndrome" also results in the Die Hard mentality.

"I'm a Democrat; Democrats are the only ones that can fix what's wrong with our country. So let's elect every Democrat candidate we can."

Or

"Democrats are the best they can do know wrong; I will only vote for a Democrat."

Unfortunately I have members of my family that are "Dyed in the wool" party thinkers. They will only vote for one party candidate. They cannot admit when their Candidate or Party makes a mistake and cannot listen to reasonable objections. At one time I myself was that way too. But then I started to look deeper into who I was voting for and why I wanted to vote for them.

Ok before I go too much further I need to tell you something. Not that I expect that anyone will care much, but this is how I have voted for President since I was able to vote.

- 1992 William Clinton (D)
- 1996 Ross Perot (I or Reform Party)
- 2000 George W Bush (R)
- 2004 George W Bush (R) *was seriously considering John Kerry but changed at the end due to remarks he said.*
- 2008 John McCain (R) *was more scared of Obama's VP candidate than of Obama.*

So why do I vote like I do because I vote based on issues and how candidates stand on those issues. I remember once in while living in Montana we were voting for a state representative and one of the issues was gun control. Now I am one who is for gun control **to a point**. Everybody knows **Democrats** want **more** gun control and **Republicans** want **less** Gun control. So the logical thought would be I would vote for the Republican candidate. But while researching the Candidate's I learned that the Republican Candidate was for strict gun control measures. While the Democratic candidate was for fewer, better and less strict gun control policies. Needless to say I voted for the Democratic Candidate.

I think that the labels Right Wing, Left Wing, Republican, Democrat, and Independent are just labels. In this day and age where everybody is worried about being politically correct and get away from using labels to group people we still do it in politics. I am not a Republican, I am not a Democrat, but I do however share some Democrat views and some Republican views.

Chapter 5

Lobbyists

So let's talk about the other thing that influences politics as a whole. That would be lobbyists. Lobbying is the act of attempting to influence decisions made by officials in the government, most often legislators or members of regulatory agencies. Lobbying is done by many different types of people and organized groups, including individuals, corporations, fellow legislators, government officials, or advocacy groups.

Lobbying in the United States is typically a paid activity in which special interests hire well-connected professional advocates to argue for or against specific legislation in Congress. This is a very controversial practice among the American public, and frequently misunderstood. Despite of the extensive rules that lobbyists must follow many people see the act of lobbying as corrupt. The act of lobbying has been interpreted by the Supreme Court as free speech and is protected by the US Constitution.

Lobbying activity rules require extensive disclosure the problem is most people don't know where or how to get it. Currently it seems that much of the lobbying is done by corporations though a wide variety of coalitions representing diverse groups. Lobbying happens at every level of government, including federal, state, county, municipal, and even local governments. In Washington DC it is believed that there is over 12,000 Lobbyists.

One of the favorite tactics that lobbyists like to use is the re-election campaign fund. This is the practice of donating money to the re-election campaign funds of legislators in the hopes that they will return the favor in cutting certain lines in a bill or changing parts to make it favorable to the contributors. For example back in 2009 when congress was working on the Dodd-Frank Act (banking reform). Lobbyists for the Banking Industry donated millions of dollars into the re-election campaign funds of several congressmen, as well as every congressman on the Senate Banking Committee. The result was that the Dodd-Frank Act ended up coming out of committee and favoring the banks more than it favored the consumers.

According to OpenSecrets.org, the following data was recorded by the Senate Office of Public Records. The top 10 industries for 2009 were:

Pharmaceuticals/Health Products - $199,323,702

Insurance - $122,065,251

Oil & Gas - $120,669,855

Electric Utilities - $108,163,536

Business Associations - $92,696,817

Computers/Internet - $88,847,937

Misc. Manufacturing & Distributing - $84,363,782

TV/Movies/Music - $77,861,927

Hospitals/Nursing Homes - $77,465,842

Education - $73,913,389

If we add those numbers up we get a total amount of $1,045,372,038. That is right over one billion dollars in money lobbyist gave to Congress.

Not all of this money goes just into re-election campaign funds some goes into pet projects in the home states of congressmen as well. Because of the General Gift Rule Provision no congressman can just take the money into their pocket. That is the reason that it has to be made as a donation to a campaign fund or as a gift to a pet project.

Chapter 6

So now what!

"Politicians are a lot like diapers. They should be changed frequently, and for the same reason."

-Benjamin Franklin-

I really enjoy the quote above. Yes it is actually a true quote from Benjamin Franklin one of our founding fathers. But even more so, it is so true. I am a very big supporter of term limits for all of Congress. House of Representatives and Senate should be limited to only two terms. Just like the President. We need to get the career politician out of politics. It is a well-known fact that many of these career politicians only continue to get re-elected because it is their name that is well known or because they spent more money on advertising than their rival.

However sitting back and hoping and wishing are not going to get it done. Change only happens when we make it happen. Someone told me one day that they hate getting old and will never retire. When I asked them why they would never want retire. The answer really blew me away. It was because he was worried Social Security would be gone. When I asked why he thought that way, he said "Because the Government always uses Social Security as a Piggy Bank, and they never pay the money back into it."

I never thought about that before till then. Then I realized something that probably no Congressman has ever thought about. That is what they need to be hearing. We elect our congressmen to do what is best for us in Washington DC. They need to know what we want done. The only way they are going to know that is if we tell them. How are we supposed to tell them? Write letters and emails, make your concerns heard. Tell them what you think, because if you aren't telling them. You can bet that someone else is telling them what you think. After all the NRA pays lobbyists thousands of dollars a year to tell your congressmen you don't need or want any gun control laws at all. Other lobbyists are getting paid to tell them you don't want fluoride in your drinking water, or that you don't really need help paying for health insurance.

Now I don't know about you but I certainly don't like the Idea of having someone else speak for me. I write my Senator and Congressmen several times a year. I send emails and letters, and I get responses. I'm not saying that everybody needs to write letters if you don't want to, but get involved there are groups of people that have the same views you do and they need your help. Get out participate, or if nothing else make your voice heard. Do you think the government should help fund more research to help find a cure for Parkinson's, or Cancer? Tell your congressman. Should we support more research to get up off of Fossil fuels? Tell your Senator. Do you believe we should stop giving other countries free aid money without some returns? Let them know. After all it is your government. Our founding fathers said it best...

A government of the people, by the people, for the people.

Appendix A

The Bill of Rights: A Transcription

Congress of the United States
begun and held at the City of New-York, on
Wednesday the fourth of March, one thousand seven hundred and
eighty nine.

THE Conventions of a number of the States, having at the time of their adopting the Constitution, expressed a desire, in order to prevent misconstruction or abuse of its powers, that further declaratory and restrictive clauses should be added: And as extending the ground of public confidence in the Government, will best ensure the beneficent ends of its institution.

RESOLVED by the Senate and House of Representatives of the United States of America, in Congress assembled, two thirds of both Houses concurring, that the following Articles be proposed to the Legislatures of the several States, as amendments to the Constitution of the United States, all, or any of which Articles, when ratified by three fourths of the said Legislatures, to be valid to all intents and purposes, as part of the said Constitution; viz.

ARTICLES in addition to, and Amendment of the Constitution of the United States of America, proposed by Congress, and ratified by the Legislatures of the several States, pursuant to the fifth Article of the original Constitution.

Amendment I

Congress shall make no law respecting an establishment of religion, or prohibiting the free exercise thereof; or abridging the freedom of speech, or of the press; or the right of the people peaceably to assemble, and to petition the Government for a redress of grievances.

Amendment II

A well regulated Militia, being necessary to the security of a free State, the right of the people to keep and bear Arms, shall not be infringed

Amendment III

No Soldier shall, in time of peace be quartered in any house, without the consent of the Owner, nor in time of war, but in a manner to be prescribed by law.

Amendment IV

The right of the people to be secure in their persons, houses, papers, and effects, against unreasonable searches and seizures, shall not be violated, and no Warrants shall issue, but upon probable cause, supported by Oath or affirmation, and particularly describing the place to be searched, and the persons or things to be seized.

Amendment V

No person shall be held to answer for a capital, or otherwise infamous crime, unless on a presentment or indictment of a Grand Jury, except in cases arising in the land or naval forces, or in the Militia, when in actual service in time of War or public danger; nor shall any person be subject for the same offence to be twice put in jeopardy of life or limb; nor shall be compelled in any criminal case to be a witness against himself, nor be deprived of life, liberty, or property, without due process of law; nor shall private property be taken for public use, without just compensation.

Amendment VI

In all criminal prosecutions, the accused shall enjoy the right to a speedy and public trial, by an impartial jury of the State and district wherein the crime shall have been committed, which district shall have been previously ascertained by law, and to be informed of the nature and cause of the accusation; to be confronted with the witnesses against him; to have compulsory process for obtaining witnesses in his favor, and to have the Assistance of Counsel for his defense.

Amendment VII

In Suits at common law, where the value in controversy shall exceed twenty dollars, the right of trial by jury shall be preserved, and no fact tried by a jury, shall be otherwise re-examined in any Court of the United States, than according to the rules of the common law.

Amendment VIII

Excessive bail shall not be required, nor excessive fines imposed, nor cruel and unusual punishments inflicted.

Amendment IX

The enumeration in the Constitution, of certain rights, shall not be construed to deny or disparage others retained by the people.

Amendment X

The powers not delegated to the United States by the Constitution, nor prohibited by it to the States, are reserved to the States respectively, or to the people.

Amendment XI

Passed by Congress March 4, 1794. Ratified February 7, 1795.

The Judicial power of the United States shall not be construed to extend to any suit in law or equity, commenced or prosecuted against one of the United States by Citizens of another State, or by Citizens or Subjects of any Foreign State.

Amendment XII
Passed by Congress December 9, 1803. Ratified June 15, 1804.

The Electors shall meet in their respective states and vote by ballot for President and Vice-President, one of whom, at least, shall not be an inhabitant of the same state with themselves; they shall name in their ballots the person voted for as President, and in distinct ballots the person voted for as Vice-President, and they shall make distinct lists of all persons voted for as President, and of all persons voted for as Vice-President, and of the number of votes for each, which lists they shall sign and certify, and transmit sealed to the seat of the government of the United States, directed to the President of the Senate; -- the President of the Senate shall, in the presence of the Senate and House of Representatives, open all the certificates and the votes shall then be counted; -- The person having the greatest number of votes for President, shall be the President, if such number be a majority of the whole number of Electors appointed; and if no person have such majority, then from the persons having the highest numbers not exceeding three on the list of those voted for as President, the House of Representatives shall choose immediately, by ballot, the President. But in choosing the President, the votes shall be taken by states, the representation from each state having one vote; a quorum for this purpose shall consist of a member or members from two-thirds of the states, and a majority of all the states shall be necessary to a choice. [And if the House of Representatives shall not choose a President whenever the right of choice shall devolve upon them, before the fourth day of March next following, then the Vice-President shall act as President, as in case of the death or other constitutional disability of the President. The person having the greatest number of votes as Vice-President, shall be the Vice-President, if such number be a majority of the whole number of Electors appointed, and if no person have a majority, then from the two highest numbers on the list, the Senate shall choose the Vice-President; a quorum for the purpose shall consist of two-thirds of the whole number of Senators, and a majority of the whole number shall be necessary to a choice. But no person constitutionally ineligible to the office of President shall be eligible to that of Vice-President of the United States.

Amendment XIII
Passed by Congress January 31, 1865. Ratified December 6, 1865.

Section 1.

Neither slavery nor involuntary servitude, except as a punishment for crime whereof the party shall have been duly convicted, shall exist within the United States, or any place subject to their jurisdiction.

Section 2.

Congress shall have power to enforce this article by appropriate legislation.

Amendment XIV
Passed by Congress June 13, 1866. Ratified July 9, 1868.

Section 1.

All persons born or naturalized in the United States, and subject to the jurisdiction thereof, are citizens of the United States and of the State wherein they reside. No State shall make or enforce any law which shall abridge the privileges or immunities of citizens of the United States; nor shall any State deprive any person of life, liberty, or property, without due process of law; nor deny to any person within its jurisdiction the equal protection of the laws.

Section 2.

Representatives shall be apportioned among the several States according to their respective numbers, counting the whole number of persons in each State, excluding Indians not taxed. But when the right to vote at any election for the choice of electors for President and Vice-President of the United States, Representatives in Congress, the Executive and Judicial officers of a State, or the members of the Legislature thereof, is denied to any of the male inhabitants of such State, being twenty-one years of age,* and citizens of the United States, or in any way abridged, except for participation in rebellion, or other crime, the basis of representation therein shall be reduced in the proportion which the number of such male citizens shall bear to the whole number of male citizens twenty-one years of age in such State.

Section 3.

No person shall be a Senator or Representative in Congress, or elector of President and Vice-President, or hold any office, civil or military, under the United States, or under any State, who, having previously taken an oath, as a member of Congress, or as an officer of the United States, or as a member of any State legislature, or as an executive or judicial officer of any State, to support the Constitution of the United States, shall have engaged in insurrection or rebellion against the same, or given aid or comfort to the enemies thereof. But Congress may by a vote of two-thirds of each House, remove such disability.

Section 4.

The validity of the public debt of the United States, authorized by law, including debts incurred for payment of pensions and bounties for services in suppressing insurrection or rebellion, shall not be questioned. But neither the United States nor any State shall assume or pay any debt or obligation incurred in aid of insurrection or rebellion against the United States, or any claim for the loss or emancipation of any slave; but all such debts, obligations and claims shall be held illegal and void.

Section 5.

The Congress shall have the power to enforce, by appropriate legislation, the provisions of this article.

Amendment XV
Passed by Congress February 26, 1869. Ratified February 3, 1870.

Section 1.

The right of citizens of the United States to vote shall not be denied or abridged by the United States or by any State on account of race, color, or previous condition of servitude--

Section 2.

The Congress shall have the power to enforce this article by appropriate legislation.

Amendment XVI
Passed by Congress July 2, 1909. Ratified February 3, 1913.

The Congress shall have power to lay and collect taxes on incomes, from whatever source derived, without apportionment among the several States, and without regard to any census or enumeration.

Amendment XVII

Passed by Congress May 13, 1912. Ratified April 8, 1913.

The Senate of the United States shall be composed of two Senators from each State, elected by the people thereof, for six years; and each Senator shall have one vote. The electors in each State shall have the qualifications requisite for electors of the most numerous branch of the State legislatures.

When vacancies happen in the representation of any State in the Senate, the executive authority of such State shall issue writs of election to fill such vacancies: Provided, That the legislature of any State may empower the executive thereof to make temporary appointments until the people fill the vacancies by election as the legislature may direct.

This amendment shall not be so construed as to affect the election or term of any Senator chosen before it becomes valid as part of the Constitution.

Amendment XVIII

Passed by Congress December 18, 1917. Ratified January 16, 1919. Repealed by amendment 21.

Section 1.

After one year from the ratification of this article the manufacture, sale, or transportation of intoxicating liquors within, the importation thereof into, or the exportation thereof from the United States and all territory subject to the jurisdiction thereof for beverage purposes is hereby prohibited.

Section 2.

The Congress and the several States shall have concurrent power to enforce this article by appropriate legislation.

Section 3.

This article shall be inoperative unless it shall have been ratified as an amendment to the Constitution by the legislatures of the several States, as provided in the Constitution, within seven years from the date of the submission hereof to the States by the Congress.

Amendment XIX
Passed by Congress June 4, 1919. Ratified August 18, 1920.

The right of citizens of the United States to vote shall not be denied or abridged by the United States or by any State on account of sex.
Congress shall have power to enforce this article by appropriate legislation.

Amendment XX
Passed by Congress March 2, 1932. Ratified January 23, 1933.

Section 1.

The terms of the President and the Vice President shall end at noon on the 20th day of January, and the terms of Senators and Representatives at noon on the 3d day of January, of the years in which such terms would have ended if this article had not been ratified; and the terms of their successors shall then begin.

Section 2.

The Congress shall assemble at least once in every year, and such meeting shall begin at noon on the 3d day of January, unless they shall by law appoint a different day.

Section 3.

If, at the time fixed for the beginning of the term of the President, the President elect shall have died, the Vice President elect shall become President. If a President shall not have been chosen before the time fixed for the beginning of his term, or if the President elect shall have failed to qualify, then the Vice President elect shall act as President until a President shall have qualified; and the Congress may by law provide for the case wherein neither a President elect nor a Vice President shall have qualified, declaring who shall then act as President, or the manner in which one who is to act shall be selected, and such person shall act accordingly until a President or Vice President shall have qualified.

Section 4.

The Congress may by law provide for the case of the death of any of the persons from whom the House of Representatives may choose a President whenever the right of choice shall have devolved upon them, and for the case of the death of any of the persons from whom the Senate may choose a Vice President whenever the right of choice shall have devolved upon them.

Section 5.

Sections 1 and 2 shall take effect on the 15th day of October following the ratification of this article.

Section 6.

This article shall be inoperative unless it shall have been ratified as an amendment to the Constitution by the legislatures of three-fourths of the several States within seven years from the date of its submission.

Amendment XXI

Passed by Congress February 20, 1933. Ratified December 5, 1933.

Section 1.

The eighteenth article of amendment to the Constitution of the United States is hereby repealed.

Section 2.

The transportation or importation into any State, Territory, or Possession of the United States for delivery or use therein of intoxicating liquors, in violation of the laws thereof, is hereby prohibited.

Section 3.

This article shall be inoperative unless it shall have been ratified as an amendment to the Constitution by conventions in the several States, as provided in the Constitution, within seven years from the date of the submission hereof to the States by the Congress.

Amendment XXII
Passed by Congress March 21, 1947. Ratified February 27, 1951.

Section 1.

No person shall be elected to the office of the President more than twice, and no person who has held the office of President, or acted as President, for more than two years of a term to which some other person was elected President shall be elected to the office of President more than once. But this Article shall not apply to any person holding the office of President when this Article was proposed by Congress, and shall not prevent any person who may be holding the office of President, or acting as President, during the term within which this Article becomes operative from holding the office of President or acting as President during the remainder of such term.

Section 2.

This article shall be inoperative unless it shall have been ratified as an amendment to the Constitution by the legislatures of three-fourths of the several States within seven years from the date of its submission to the States by the Congress.

Amendment XXIII
Passed by Congress June 16, 1960. Ratified March 29, 1961.

Section 1.

The District constituting the seat of Government of the United States shall appoint in such manner as Congress may direct:

A number of electors of President and Vice President equal to the whole number of Senators and Representatives in Congress to which the District would be entitled if it were a State, but in no event more than the least populous State; they shall be in addition to those appointed by the States, but they shall be considered, for the purposes of the election of President and Vice President, to be electors appointed by a State; and they shall meet in the District and perform such duties as provided by the twelfth article of amendment.

Section 2.

The Congress shall have power to enforce this article by appropriate legislation.

Amendment XXIV
Passed by Congress August 27, 1962. Ratified January 23, 1964.

Section 1.

The right of citizens of the United States to vote in any primary or other election for President or Vice President, for electors for President or Vice President, or for Senator or Representative in Congress, shall not be denied or abridged by the United States or any State by reason of failure to pay poll tax or other tax.

Section 2.

The Congress shall have power to enforce this article by appropriate legislation.

Amendment XXV
Passed by Congress July 6, 1965. Ratified February 10, 1967.

Section 1.

In case of the removal of the President from office or of his death or resignation, the Vice President shall become President.

Section 2.

Whenever there is a vacancy in the office of the Vice President, the President shall nominate a Vice President who shall take office upon confirmation by a majority vote of both Houses of Congress.

Section 3.

Whenever the President transmits to the President pro tempore of the Senate and the Speaker of the House of Representatives his written declaration that he is unable to discharge the powers and duties of his office, and until he transmits to them a written declaration to the contrary, such powers and duties shall be discharged by the Vice President as Acting President.

Section 4.

Whenever the Vice President and a majority of either the principal officers of the executive departments or of such other body as Congress may by law provide, transmit to the President pro tempore of the Senate and the Speaker of the House of Representatives their written declaration that the President is unable to discharge the powers and duties of his office, the Vice President shall immediately assume the powers and duties of the office as Acting President.

Thereafter, when the President transmits to the President pro tempore of the Senate and the Speaker of the House of Representatives his written declaration that no inability exists, he shall resume the powers and duties of his office unless the Vice President and a majority of either the principal officers of the executive department or of such other body as Congress may by law provide, transmit within four days to the President pro tempore of the Senate and the Speaker of the House of Representatives their written declaration that the President is unable to discharge the powers and duties of his office. Thereupon Congress shall decide the issue, assembling within forty-eight hours for that purpose if not in session. If the Congress, within twenty-one days after receipt of the latter written declaration, or, if Congress is not in session, within twenty-one days after Congress is required to assemble, determines by two-thirds vote of both Houses that the President is unable to discharge the powers and duties of his office, the Vice President shall continue to discharge the same as Acting President; otherwise, the President shall resume the powers and duties of his office.

Amendment XXVI

Passed by Congress March 23, 1971. Ratified July 1, 1971.

Section 1.

The right of citizens of the United States, who are eighteen years of age or older, to vote shall not be denied or abridged by the United States or by any State on account of age.

Section 2.

The Congress shall have power to enforce this article by appropriate legislation.

Amendment XXVII

Originally proposed Sept. 25, 1789. Ratified May 7, 1992.

No law, varying the compensation for the services of the Senators and Representatives, shall take effect, until an election of representatives shall have intervened.[3]

---

[3] Source: www.archives.gov

Appendix B

The Declaration of Independence: A Transcription

IN CONGRESS, July 4, 1776.

The unanimous Declaration of the thirteen united States of America,

When in the Course of human events, it becomes necessary for one people to dissolve the political bands which have connected them with another, and to assume among the powers of the earth, the separate and equal station to which the Laws of Nature and of Nature's God entitle them, a decent respect to the opinions of mankind requires that they should declare the causes which impel them to the separation.

We hold these truths to be self-evident, that all men are created equal, that they are endowed by their Creator with certain unalienable Rights, that among these are Life, Liberty and the pursuit of Happiness.--That to secure these rights, Governments are instituted among Men, deriving their just powers from the consent of the governed, --That whenever any Form of Government becomes destructive of these ends, it is the Right of the People to alter or to abolish it, and to institute new Government, laying its foundation on such principles and organizing its powers in such form, as to them shall seem most likely to effect their Safety and Happiness. Prudence, indeed, will dictate that Governments long established should not be changed for light and transient causes; and accordingly all experience hath shewn, that mankind are more disposed to suffer, while evils are sufferable, than to right themselves by abolishing the forms to which they are accustomed. But when a long train of abuses and usurpations, pursuing invariably the same Object evinces a design to reduce them under absolute Despotism, it is their right, it is their duty, to throw off such Government, and to provide new Guards for their future security.--Such has been the patient sufferance of these Colonies; and such is now the necessity which constrains them to alter their former Systems of Government. The history of the present King of Great Britain is a history of repeated injuries and usurpations, all having in direct object the establishment of an absolute Tyranny over these States. To prove this, let Facts be submitted to a candid world.

He has refused his Assent to Laws, the most wholesome and necessary for the public good.
He has forbidden his Governors to pass Laws of immediate and pressing importance, unless suspended in their operation till his Assent should be obtained; and when so suspended, he has utterly neglected to attend to them.

He has refused to pass other Laws for the accommodation of large districts of people, unless those people would relinquish the right of Representation in the Legislature, a right inestimable to them and formidable to tyrants only.

He has called together legislative bodies at places unusual, uncomfortable, and distant from the depository of their public Records, for the sole purpose of fatiguing them into compliance with his measures.

He has dissolved Representative Houses repeatedly, for opposing with manly firmness his invasions on the rights of the people.

He has refused for a long time, after such dissolutions, to cause others to be elected; whereby the Legislative powers, incapable of Annihilation, have returned to the People at large for their exercise; the State remaining in the mean time exposed to all the dangers of invasion from without, and convulsions within.

He has endeavoured to prevent the population of these States; for that purpose obstructing the Laws for Naturalization of Foreigners; refusing to pass others to encourage their migrations hither, and raising the conditions of new Appropriations of Lands.

He has obstructed the Administration of Justice, by refusing his Assent to Laws for establishing Judiciary powers.

He has made Judges dependent on his Will alone, for the tenure of their offices, and the amount and payment of their salaries.

He has erected a multitude of New Offices, and sent hither swarms of Officers to harrass our people, and eat out their substance.

He has kept among us, in times of peace, Standing Armies without the Consent of our legislatures.

He has affected to render the Military independent of and superior to the Civil power.

He has combined with others to subject us to a jurisdiction foreign to our constitution, and unacknowledged by our laws; giving his Assent to their Acts of pretended Legislation:

For Quartering large bodies of armed troops among us:

For protecting them, by a mock Trial, from punishment for any Murders which they should commit on the Inhabitants of these States:

For cutting off our Trade with all parts of the world:

For imposing Taxes on us without our Consent:

For depriving us in many cases, of the benefits of Trial by Jury:

For transporting us beyond Seas to be tried for pretended offences

For abolishing the free System of English Laws in a neighbouring Province, establishing therein an Arbitrary government, and enlarging its Boundaries so as to render it at once an example and fit instrument for introducing the same absolute rule into these Colonies:

For taking away our Charters, abolishing our most valuable Laws, and altering fundamentally the Forms of our Governments:

For suspending our own Legislatures, and declaring themselves invested with power to legislate for us in all cases whatsoever.

He has abdicated Government here, by declaring us out of his Protection and waging War against us.

He has plundered our seas, ravaged our Coasts, burnt our towns, and destroyed the lives of our people.

He is at this time transporting large Armies of foreign Mercenaries to compleat the works of death, desolation and tyranny, already begun with circumstances of Cruelty & perfidy scarcely paralleled in the most barbarous ages, and totally unworthy the Head of a civilized nation.

He has constrained our fellow Citizens taken Captive on the high Seas to bear Arms against their Country, to become the executioners of their friends and Brethren, or to fall themselves by their Hands.

He has excited domestic insurrections amongst us, and has endeavoured to bring on the inhabitants of our frontiers, the merciless Indian Savages, whose known rule of warfare, is an undistinguished destruction of all ages, sexes and conditions.

In every stage of these Oppressions We have Petitioned for Redress in the most humble terms: Our repeated Petitions have been answered only by repeated injury. A Prince whose character is thus marked by every act which may define a Tyrant, is unfit to be the ruler of a free people.

Nor have We been wanting in attentions to our Brittish brethren. We have warned them from time to time of attempts by their legislature to extend an unwarrantable jurisdiction over us. We have reminded them of the circumstances of our emigration and settlement here. We have appealed to their native justice and magnanimity, and we have conjured them by the ties of our common kindred to disavow these usurpations, which, would inevitably interrupt our connections and correspondence. They too have been deaf to the voice of justice and of consanguinity. We must, therefore, acquiesce in the necessity, which denounces our Separation, and hold them, as we hold the rest of mankind, Enemies in War, in Peace Friends.

We, therefore, the Representatives of the united States of America, in General Congress, Assembled, appealing to the Supreme Judge of the world for the rectitude of our intentions, do, in the Name, and by Authority of the good People of these Colonies, solemnly publish and declare, That these United Colonies are, and of Right ought to be Free and Independent States; that they are Absolved from all Allegiance to the British Crown, and that all political connection between them and the State of Great Britain, is and ought to be totally dissolved; and that as Free and Independent States, they have full Power to levy War, conclude Peace, contract Alliances, establish Commerce, and to do all other Acts and Things which Independent States may of right do. And for the support of this Declaration, with a firm reliance on the protection of divine Providence, we mutually pledge to each other our Lives, our Fortunes and our sacred Honor.[4]

---

[4] Source: www.archives.gov

www.ingramcontent.com/pod-product-compliance
Lightning Source LLC
Chambersburg PA
CBHW072343290526
45794CB00002B/993